Origins

Space Holidays

and other freaky futures

Paul Mason

Contents

A changing world 2
You'll redesign your world 4
You'll be a time traveller – almost! 6
Your clothes could be really clever 8
You'll be able to print anything you want 10
You'll no longer get pocket money 12
You'll have your very own doctor 14
You won't go to school 16
You'll download data to your brain 18
You'll use micro-robots to do your dirty work 20
Your robots will begin to fight back 22
You'll eat meat grown in labs 24
Your food will improve your health 26
You'll be drinking your own wee 28
You'll never have to pester your parents for a lift 30
You'll blast into space for holidays 32
You may even be living in space 34
Future bloopers 36
Quiz of your future! 38
Glossary 39
Index 40

OXFORD
UNIVERSITY PRESS

A changing world

Imagine being a child teleported here from a time when your grandparents were children. Modern life would freak you out! Making Internet video calls, ordering online or using a satnav would beggar belief!

The world has changed a LOT in the last 60 years or so: our homes, schools, jobs, food, health and the ways we stay in touch are all very different now.

The changes are coming faster and faster, too. Text messaging, smartphones and social networks have only been around for a few years but just imagine how they would **bamboozle** a kid from the past!

It does make you wonder … what will the world be like in 60 years' time, when YOU might be a grandparent?

From gramophone to MP3

The way we listen to music has changed dramatically. Over the years music has become more and more portable.

1887
Gramophone

1962
Cassette tape player

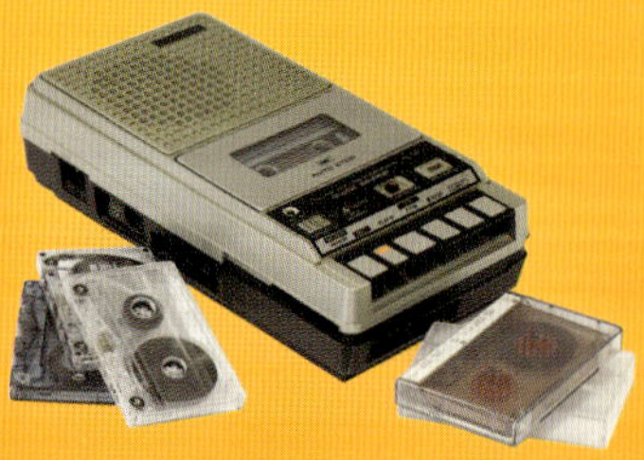

Predicting the future

All around the world **futurists** are trying to predict, yes you guessed it, exactly what the future will be like. Some of their top ideas appear in this book, but how do they come up with these predictions and determine how probable they are? The three main strategies used are:

1. Scanning: looking at news sources to identify **trends**.
2. Visioning: imagining a particular kind of future.
3. Working out how likely these possible futures are.

Cities of the future will use all kinds of new technologies.

1982
Portable CD player

1997
MP3 player

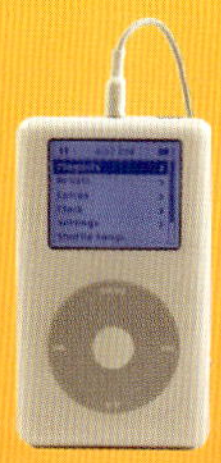

The future?
Imagine not needing a player at all – what if music could be streamed straight to an **implant** in your head?

You'll redesign your world

Imagine if you could change your bedroom to suit your mood. Just think of the possibilities: a room in an old castle would be perfect for watching scary movies; a hut on a Hawaiian beach would bring the surf to you; or how about trying to sleep in an observation post on the doorstep of a bubbling volcano?

▲ If your beach-hut bedroom gets boring – just reprogram it!

How would it work?

Every room – in fact, every *thing* – is made up of tiny units called atoms. Normally the way these atoms are joined together doesn't change. That's why the lamp beside your bed always looks the same.

The idea of a room that can change its shape is based on something called **claytronics**: tiny computer-atoms are programmed to change how they are joined to other atoms. This would mean your lamp could be a flickering torch one night and a candle in a coconut shell the next.

Why stop at bedrooms?

Claytronics could mean big changes in other areas too – not just interior design! It could allow you to immerse yourself in a video game, so that you are not only able to see and hear the action, but also feel it! People at the other end of a phone might be able to pat your arm or give you a hug, or even appear before you, a bit like a solid hologram.

With claytronics, this might all be possible. Signals from a games console could cause a claytronic suit to change its shape, so that it could squeeze your arm or tap you on the shoulder when there was something behind you in the game! Or signals from a smartphone could cause the suit to transform into your friend, so it would be like chatting in person.

Probability Rating

Successful experiments in claytronics have already been carried out. However, there is a problem: computer-atoms are currently too big for claytronics to work and, at present, they aren't as mobile as they would need to be. But if the computer-atoms can be **miniaturized** and better controlled, claytronics could happen.

▲ Imagine if characters from a game could creep up behind you! With claytronics, this could start to feel like reality.

You'll be a time traveller – almost!

Have you ever wondered what it would be like to travel back in time? Maybe you're interested in what life was like as a Roman gladiator, a Viking warrior or a Mayan noble? Perhaps you'd like to witness the first step on the Moon, or explore the Arctic?

Past Worlds™

Join the COLOSSEUM CROWDS!

Ever fancied watching gladiators battle in Ancient Rome? Past Worlds™ offers you the chance to find out what it was really like!

The Past Worlds™ body suit – in combination with our SurroundVision™ goggles – gives you the full Colosseum experience.

- Warm up as the sun rises over Rome.
- Feel nudges and shoves as other spectators find their seats.
- Hear the noise of battle as the gladiators clash.
- Don't get too close – it feels very real!

How would it work?

With this technology you might *feel* you've been to a past world – but you won't even have left town! Instead, you'll have been completely immersed in a **virtual** world. This relies on two things:

1. Realistic computer graphics seen through a pair of 3D goggles and atmospheric noise heard through headphones. These would coordinate with your movements so that as you turn your head or move around, the scene moves with you.

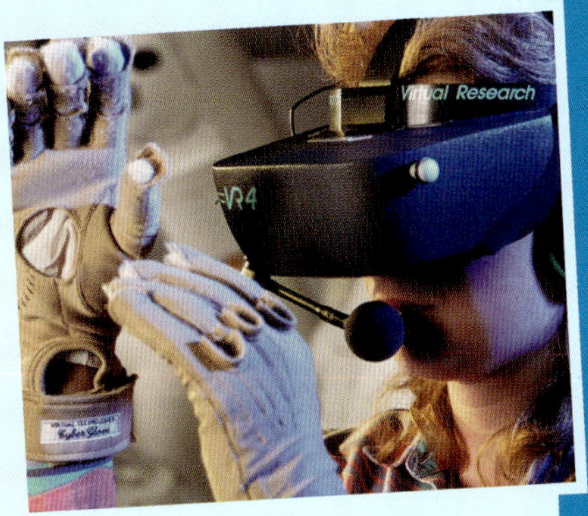

2. A full-body claytronic reality suit, which can alter its shape and temperature. This would make bumps from a jostling crowd feel real and could recreate the sensations of getting hotter, colder or even standing in the rain.

Thoughts to ponder

Perhaps, one day, you will also be able to smell and taste other worlds, adding to the intensity of the experience. It's worth remembering that, though it may feel like you've experienced a real world, it would only be a modern interpretation of that time; one that relies on people to create it, just like a computer game. Therefore it might not be as objective or accurate as you'd hope. For that, you'll just have to wait for real time travel to be invented!

Probability Rating

3D goggles already exist, claytronics systems (see pages 4–5) are being developed right now and virtual worlds are becoming more realistic every year. Just think, for example, how much more lifelike computer-game graphics have become in the last few years.

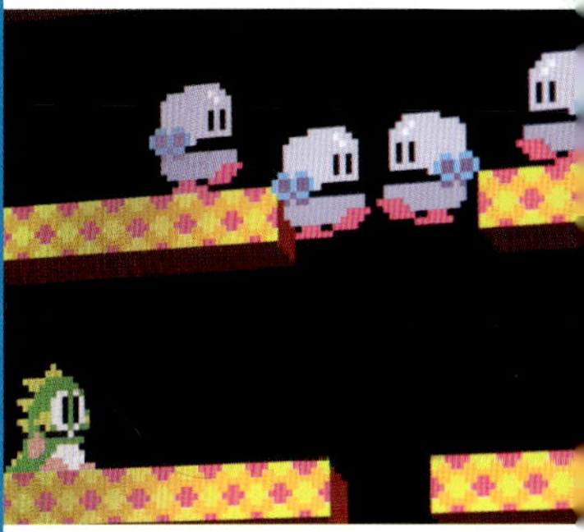

▲ In the 1980s video games were unrealistic.

▲ By the 2000s, the action was far more realistic.

Your clothes could be really clever

Imagine this. You're waiting at a bus stop, feeling a bit lonely and bored. Perhaps it's raining. Suddenly, your coat gives you a lovely, friendly hug. It cheers you up no end! That hug means someone has 'liked' your post on a social network. This is just one way fashion might be more interactive in the future.

How could my clothes be clever?

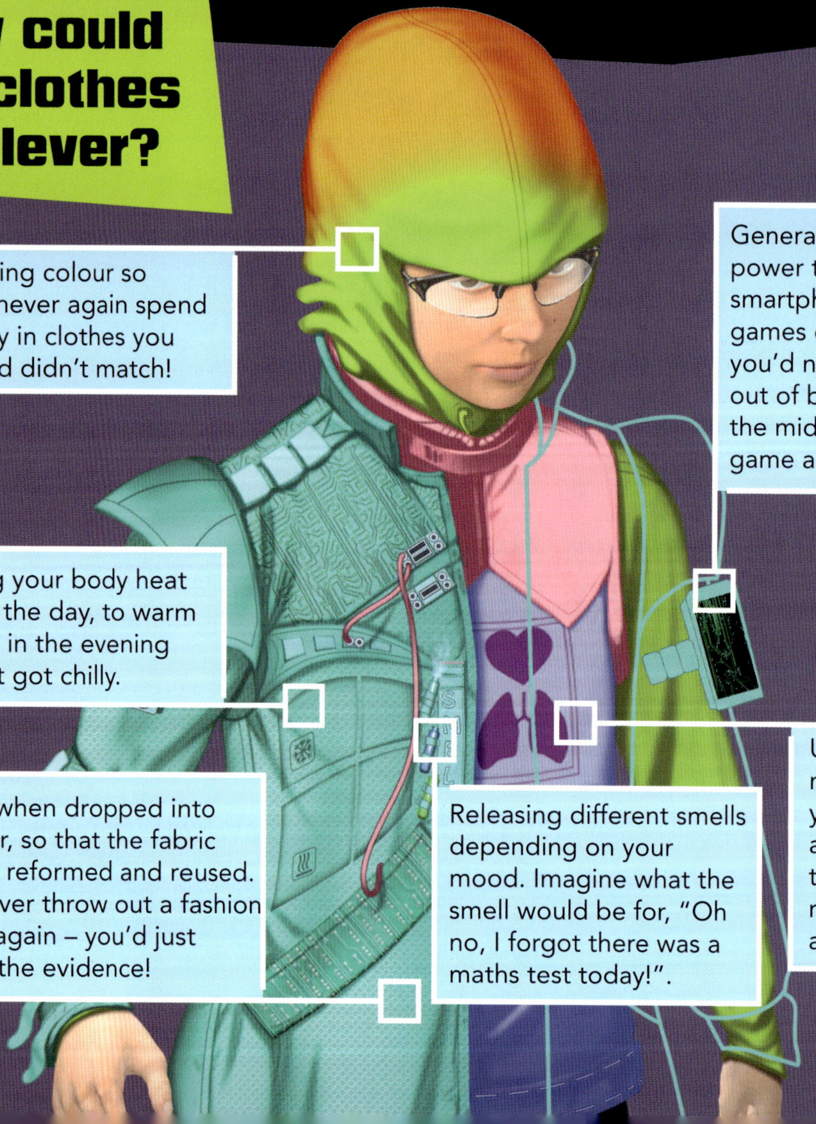

Are you there?

For the secret agents among you, clever clothes are already here. One company is already making clothes that are undetectable to **spy drones**. To shield people from a drone, the fabric masks their body heat so that the drone's **thermal** imaging cameras cannot see the wearer.

Another company has developed a fabric that bends light, making the wearer seem invisible. It is not yet known exactly how the fabric works – the makers won't divulge their secrets and the only photos of the fabric in action are mock-ups. A few top-secret military personnel are said to have witnessed the invisibility fabric in action (though no one seems able to find them!).

Probability Rating

Amazingly, coats that give you a hug have *already* been designed. In Japan, there's a coat that uses robot arms to give you a squeeze, and in the USA a jacket has been developed that inflates when someone 'likes' something on your social networking page. In the future, coats made of claytronic material could do the same job in an even more realistic way.

Freaky future!

Imagine if your clothes really could make you invisible. Would it be a good thing or is there a chance people could misuse them, such as to commit a crime?

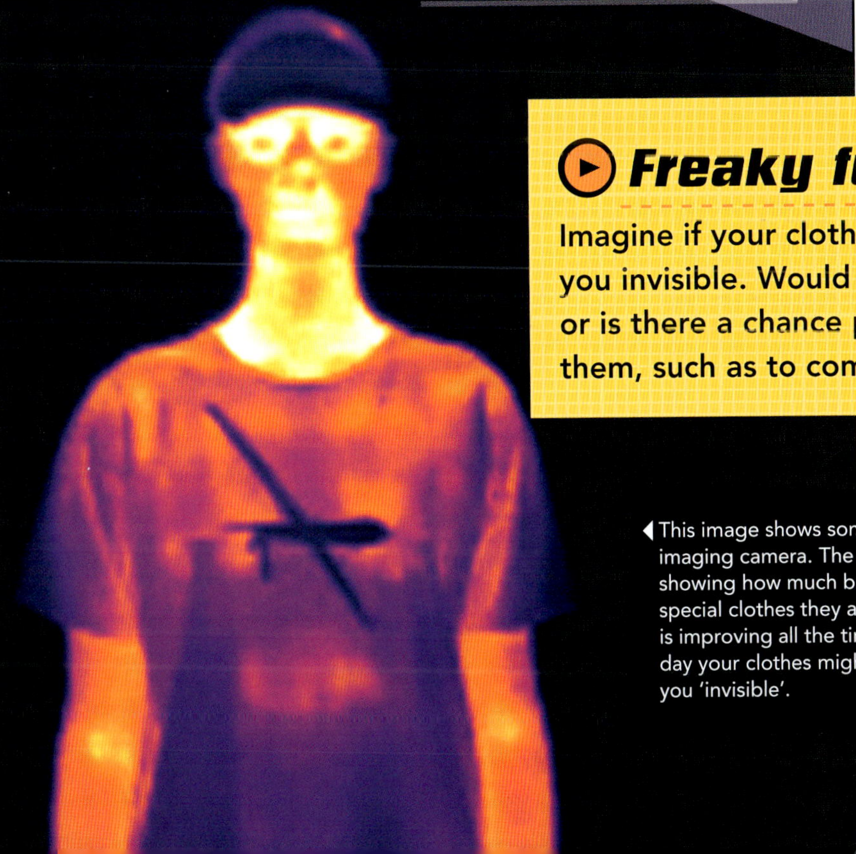

This image shows someone as seen by a thermal imaging camera. The hottest areas are in yellow, showing how much body heat is masked by the special clothes they are wearing. Technology is improving all the time so, who knows, one day your clothes might really be able to make you 'invisible'.

You'll be able to print anything you want

So you've decided your bedroom is going to be a surf shack tonight. The bed is now a hammock, the lamp is a flickering candle and the chair has become a carved log. But, disaster! Where's your surfboard? Don't worry – you can just print one!

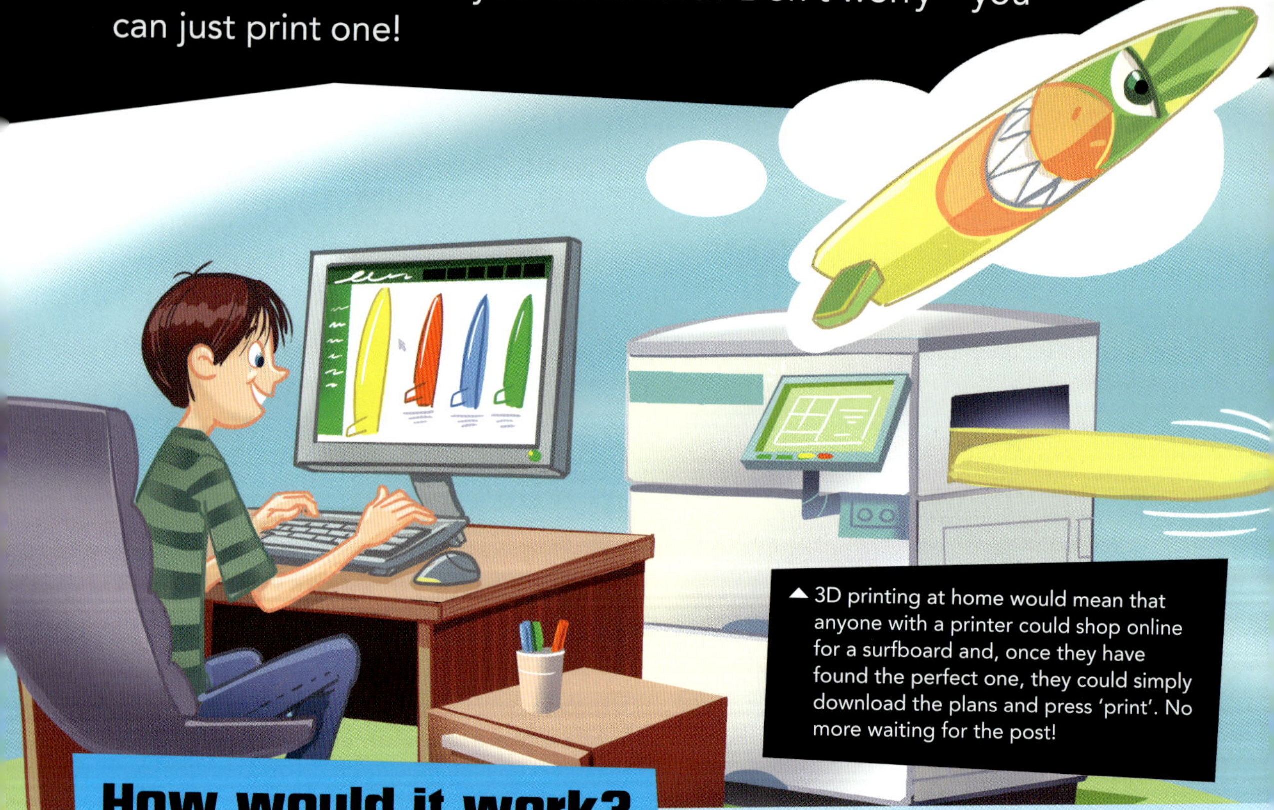

▲ 3D printing at home would mean that anyone with a printer could shop online for a surfboard and, once they have found the perfect one, they could simply download the plans and press 'print'. No more waiting for the post!

How would it work?

3D printing already exists. The printer calls up a 3D plan or model of an object and separates this model into super-thin layers. The printer then prints each layer, one after the next.

The layers can be made out of different substances, such as liquid plastic, that then hardens, or grains of material that melt and then fuse together when heated. When the layers are joined together by the printer, you are left with a real object, such as a surfboard.

Printing with your mind

Imagine being able to picture an object in your head, then print it out! It sounds weird – but the very first steps towards this vision have already been taken.

The process begins with a headset that monitors brain activity in 14 different areas. A computer records this activity and combines it with a basic framework to create a plan or model that can then be 3D printed.

The only limit is your imagination!

Probability Rating

3D printing not only could happen, it already *has*. All sorts of things have been produced using 3D printing, from the useful, to the fun, to the rather serious: spare parts for old cars, bicycles, guitars, high-heeled shoes, perfect models of steam trains and even a new jawbone for an 83-year-old woman.

It has even been suggested that 3D printing could be used to 'build' a Moon base. Instead of having to transport parts from Earth, which could be difficult and costly, the base could be designed on Earth and then printed on the Moon!

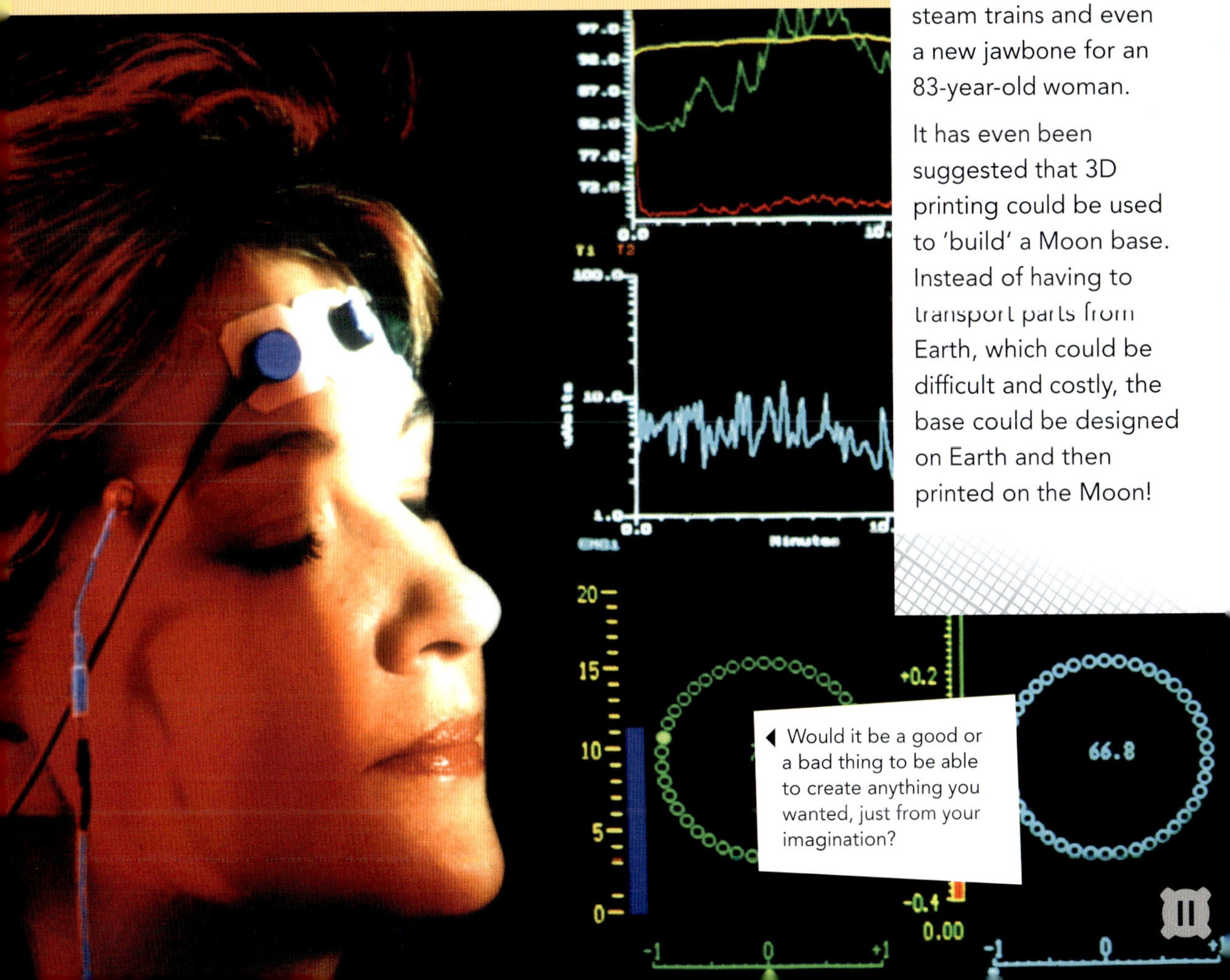

Would it be a good or a bad thing to be able to create anything you wanted, just from your imagination?

You'll no longer get pocket money

Don't panic! You'll still be able to buy things – you just won't be doing it with actual money. Instead of fumbling for the right coins, you'll just wave a hand at the checkout and computers will do the rest!

P PALM BANK CORP

Try our new high-speed payment processors!

FIRST SIX MONTHS FREE!

No more queues at the checkout – just sail through with a wave of your hand ★ No more worries about forgetting your pin or losing your card ★ Completely hygienic – no more germ-covered notes and coins

Failure to keep up payments may lead to your chip being reclaimed. Anaesthetic and surgical charges for chip reclaim may apply.

How would it work?

Rather than carrying notes and coins, people would have electronic **credit**. It would work a bit like bank cards do now, but the future version would be even easier, faster and more secure. A **microprocessor** containing personal information would be implanted in your body, allowing scanners in shops to identify you and link to your bank **account**, checking whether you have enough credit. If the answer was 'yes', the scanner would then take the payment from your account.

Thoughts to ponder

It all sounds great, doesn't it? But are there any drawbacks to this technology?

1. If your 'money' was carried in a chip under your skin, would you feel safe from thieves?
2. What would happen to people who couldn't afford the implant?
3. What if the chip **malfunctioned** – would it need to be regularly replaced and updated? Ouch!

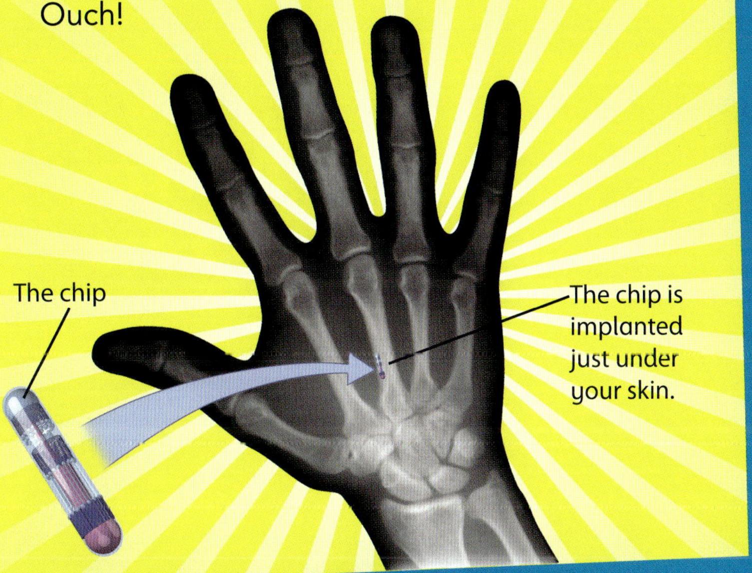

Probability Rating

Some bank cards and pre-payment cards already contain microprocessors – you just place the card on the scanner. Mobile phones can also make payments for you. An app creates a 'virtual wallet' in the phone. A chip inside the phone picks up information about the product you want to purchase and the price, then passes it on to the virtual wallet for payment.

Similar technology in a chip implanted under the skin of your hand could work in the same way – but would people be willing to take this next step?

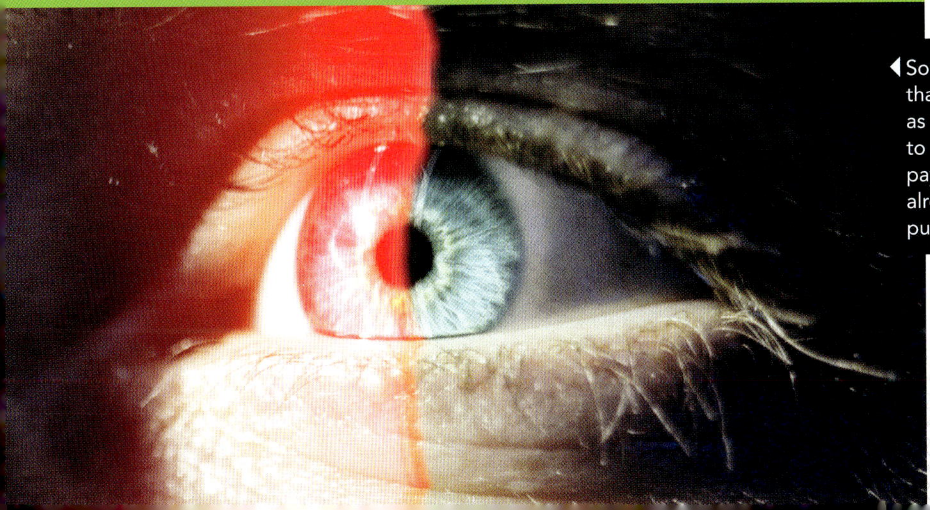

◀ Some futurists have suggested that scans of retinas – as unique as fingerprints – could be used to identify people and make payments. This technology is already in use for identification purposes.

You'll have your very own doctor

It's a rainy day, you've got a test at school, you haven't done your homework and the World Cup is on TV. What do you do? You could hold your head against the radiator and claim you've got a temperature and need to stay at home today. Unfortunately, in the future that won't work (if it ever did; and I'm sure you're too good ever to have tried it): using one little bag, adults will know the truth.

WORRIED YOUR CHILD IS ILL?

DOCTOR IN A BAG

You need GlobalHealth's new 'Doctor in a Bag'™!

3 EASY STEPS

Know in three quick and easy steps whether or not your child is ill:

1 Get your child to blow into the bag.
2 Wait three minutes.
3 Doctor in a Bag™ gives you a diagnosis.

Doctor in a Bag™ detects most major childhood diseases, so you'll know for SURE if it's safe to send your child to school or not.

How would it work?

Disease breathalysers would work by detecting the chemicals that appear in your breath when you are ill. On a simple level, they could tell you whether or not you were ill and needed to visit the doctor. On a more complex level, they might tell you *exactly* what was wrong with you and, who knows, perhaps even prescribe a treatment.

Would it be a good idea?

For many people, self-diagnosis would be a good thing. Fewer people would visit the doctor unnecessarily, meaning doctors could spend longer with patients who have potentially life-threatening illnesses. People living in remote places wouldn't have to make long journeys to the doctor, either. However, relying on such a device carries its own risks – what if it were to malfunction? Could it make a misdiagnosis if there were several symptoms to take into account?

▼ Would you trust an electronic doctor?

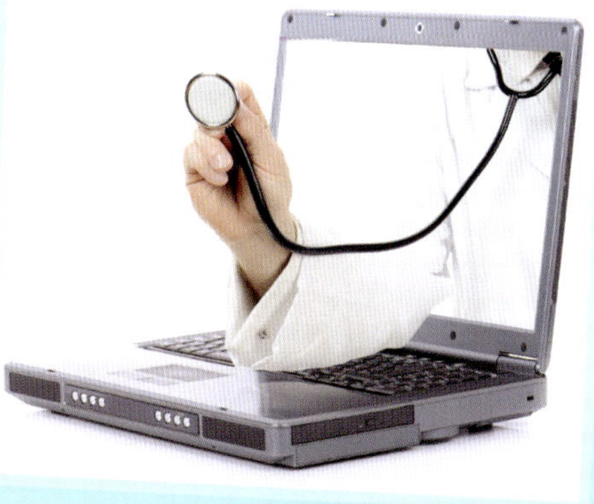

Probability Rating

Scientists already know how to tell if someone is ill by analysing their breath. In fact, a simple device to do this is likely to be available within the next few years.

Current technology can't diagnose exactly *what* is wrong with you, only that you are unwell. In the future, though, disease breathalysers will probably become more accurate and be able to diagnose serious health problems such as tuberculosis, dysentery, pneumonia or cancer.

Freaky future!

Could technology become so advanced that it could start to predict *future* illnesses? How might this affect how you live your life? Would you live more healthily to try to prevent contracting these illnesses?

You won't go to school

Imagine if you didn't have to go to school. In fact, imagine a future *without* schools! Don't get too excited, though. It wouldn't be like a long summer holiday: you'd still have to study!

Is a virtual classroom the answer?

▲ In a virtual classroom, you would interact with your classmates on screen. What would you miss about seeing them in person?

How would it work?

In this version of the future, you would learn while sitting at a computer screen at home and lessons would be taught by interactive **software**.

If you think being taught by software sounds dull and impersonal, there is hope! Many futurists think learning with computers is likely to become more game-based, so you could find yourself immersed in virtual environments, working on different challenges with people from all over the world.

Would it be a good idea?

Virtual learning would save the money currently used to build and maintain schools and employ staff. Learning software could be shared globally, giving everyone everywhere the same learning opportunities.

Of course, there are potential downsides to computer-based learning. Would you get enough exercise? Would you make as many friends? Would you learn as much? Would everyone be able to afford it? Is there a benefit to experiencing things in real life rather than in a virtual world? Would someone have to stay at home with you? Could a computer ever know you as well as your teacher does?

Probability Rating

Virtual learning technology already exists: children in isolated places, such as the Australian outback, already learn in virtual classrooms linked to computers. Currently these lessons are run by flesh-and-blood teachers, linked to their students by the Internet. But computer-only programs for studying foreign languages, exam revision, and all sorts of other learning already exist. It might not be long before people take the next step!

My view on virtual learning

I would give you 10/10. I like being taught over the computer; Laura is good, she is nice to us, talks to us, and listens to us.

by KR, Year 6 student

I would give you a 10/10, feel it has helped me, and I enjoyed it very much, Laura is nice and makes me feel comfortable.

by MH, Year 6 student

This has been a very good experience for all the children. They have been enthusiastic and they have enjoyed this new way of learning online. Laura, their tutor, has been fantastic. She has been able to engage the children with their learning and she has been very friendly and humorous in her lessons.

by staff of the Pupil Referral Unit

You'll download data to your brain

Have you ever thought that researching facts using books or a computer is just *too slow*? Then you might like this version of the future! In it, if you want to check the capital of Kyrgyzstan,* you'll just search a computer chip inside your own head. In the blink of an eye, the answer will arrive.

**It's Bishkek, by the way.*

How would it work?

Futurists think that computer implants could one day be used to boost memory capacity, so that your brain would work faster and store more information.

You would be able to carry a whole library of information with you at all times, so no more looking in books or searching online for an answer!

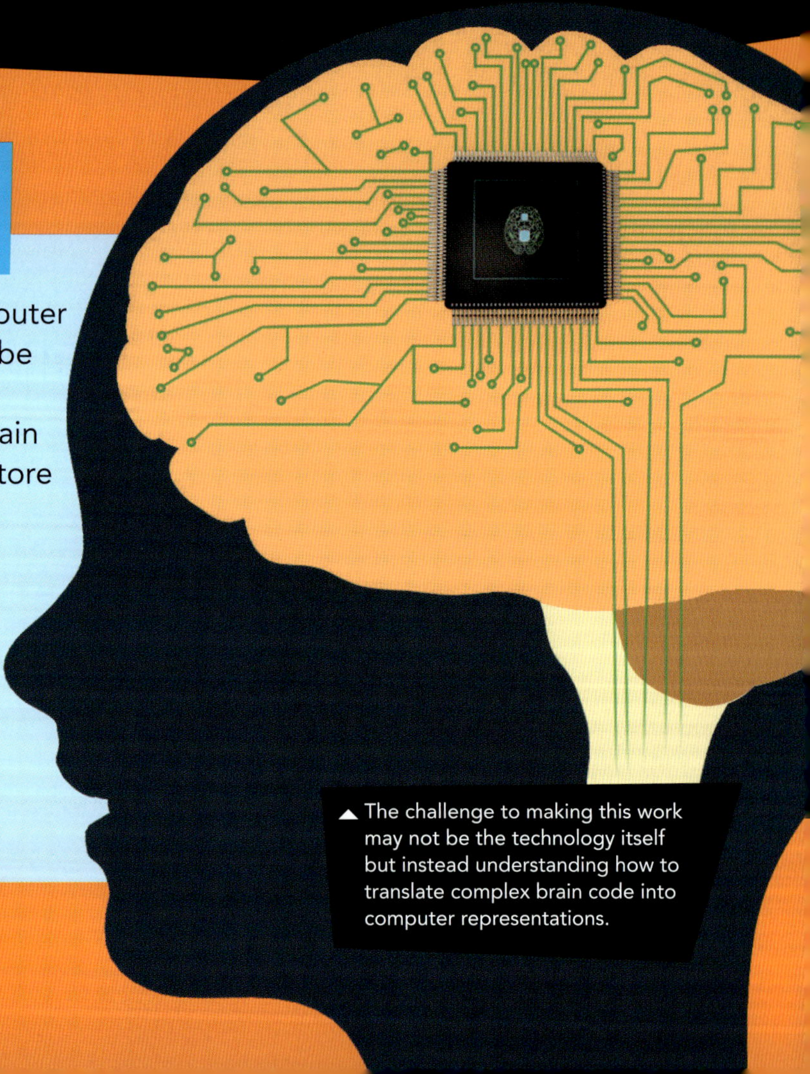

▲ The challenge to making this work may not be the technology itself but instead understanding how to translate complex brain code into computer representations.

Freaky future!

Not having to learn facts may sound great, but have a think about the downsides:

1. Would an update require brain surgery?
2. What would it be like if your friends could afford an update but you couldn't?
3. What if someone tried to hack into your memory or if you got a computer virus?

Probability Rating

BCI implant technology is improving all the time. Of course, this is a step away from implanting a computer system in someone's head but it does show that human brains can be successfully linked to computers.

Other uses of brain implants

BCI (Brain-Computer Interface) implants are already being used to help people with disabilities and have been around for a long time – the first blind person to 'see' using a BCI was in 1978. People who have been paralysed can also use brain implants to control both **prosthetic** limbs and external (unattached) robotic hands.

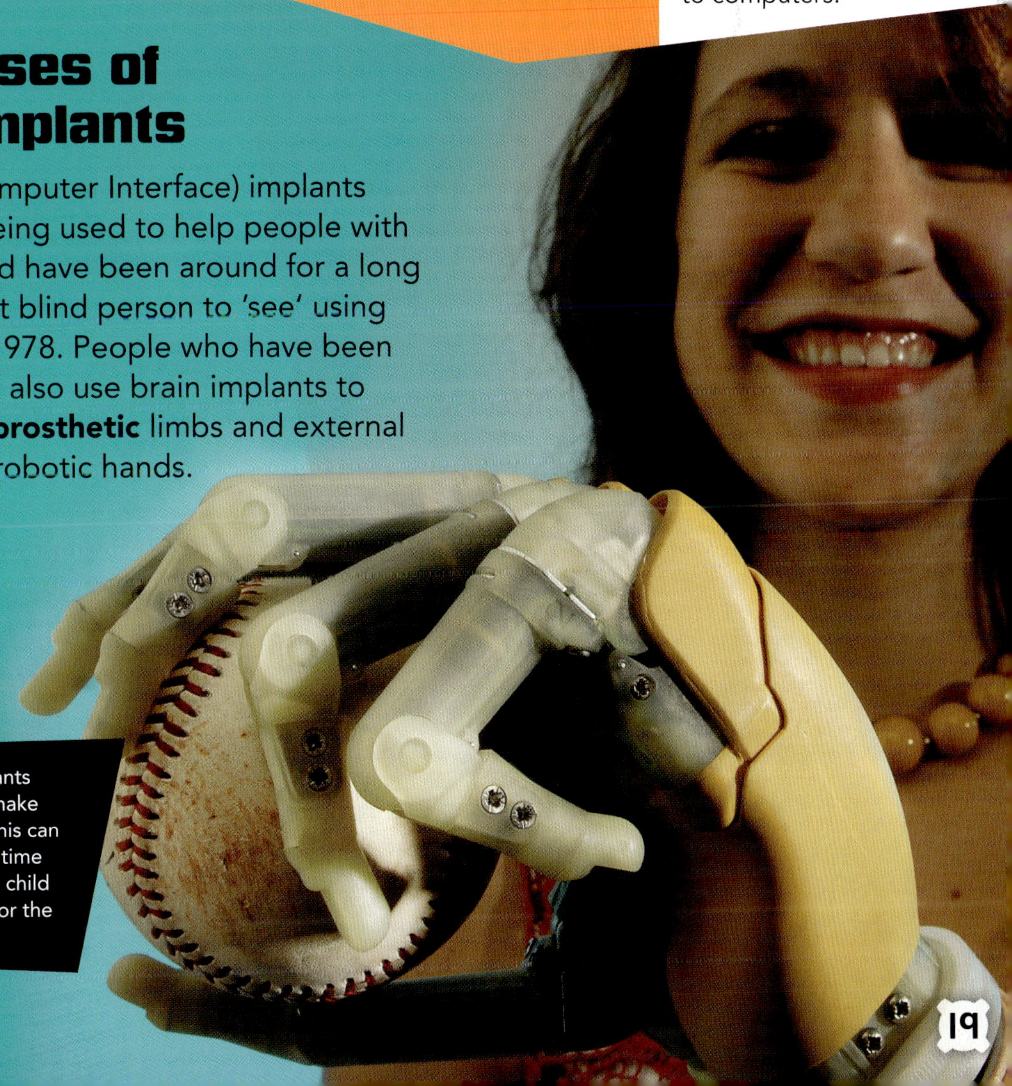

People with implants have to learn to make the limbs work. This can often take a long time – it's almost like a child learning to walk for the first time.

You'll use micro-robots to do your dirty work

Imagine a world full of robots. Not just the household helpers we'd all love to have, but micro-robots too small to see, that would help us to keep clean and stay healthy.

Robot body bugs

Most of the time we don't think about body bugs. After all, who likes to remember that there are little mites living in their eyelashes, feasting on dead skin; or **bacteria** living in their gut, helping with **digestion**; or tiny **organisms** on their skin, keeping infections at bay?

But how would you feel if some of your natural bugs were being helped by micro-robots?

▲ Nanobots will be self-replicating so engineers will need to harness and contain that capability, otherwise they could overrun the human body.

Freaky future!

Some futurists worry that nanobots could begin to consume the bodies they live inside. Far from making humans immortal, that could spell the end of the human race, destroying itself from within!

Probability Rating

Scientists are currently developing tiny robots called nanobots that are so small they would be able to swim in your bloodstream.

Scientists think that nanobots would soon be able to help doctors treat and even prevent all kinds of illnesses. They could also help control digestion, making sure we stay healthy. Some futurists predict that, by 2050, nanobots could make humans immortal.

Robotic rubbish worms

Robots won't just live on you but around you too ...

Sorting rubbish into recycling bins can be a pain but on a larger scale, what to do with all our waste is a real headache! Humans are creating more and more waste and we're running out of places to put it.

In the future, robotic earthworms may wriggle their way through our old rubbish. They could chomp up anything useful and bring it back for recycling, reducing the waste left in **landfills**.

Probability Rating

Robot worms that sort through our rubbish for useful **resources** certainly *sound* like a good idea. In fact, they were once one of the World Future Society's Top 10 predictions for the future.

A robot called BREADbot, which powers itself using food waste, has already been built. It's possible that BREADbot could one day become a rubbish-sorting robot. It could even be miniaturized to allow it to crawl into small spaces.

◀ Robotic worms could change the way we deal with our rubbish.

Your robots will begin to fight back

Everyone loves the idea of robots doing the jobs we hate. In the future, they could wash the dishes, clean your trainers, change the sheets, tidy your room – the possibilities are endless! But as robots become more advanced, perhaps they will get fed up with doing our chores. They might even be annoyed enough to start a robot rebellion!

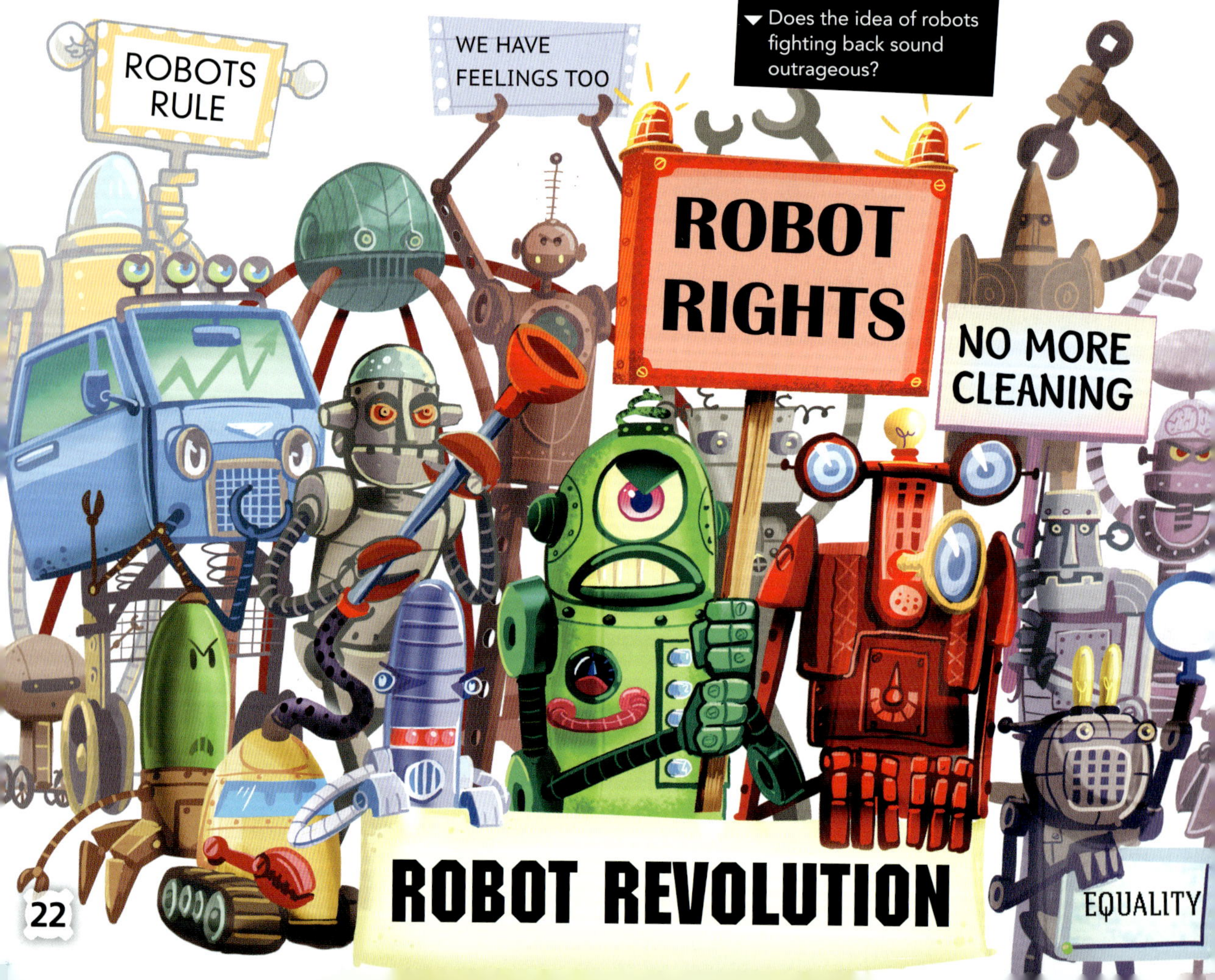

▼ Does the idea of robots fighting back sound outrageous?

How would it work?

The idea of a robot rebellion is based on two things that futurists think could happen:

1 People would become more like robots.

Robot hands, feet, arms and legs are being developed for people who were born without or who have lost limbs. One day soon, we may see the first human with robot limbs, whose brain is partly powered by a computer. On pages 18 and 19 you can read about how computers may one day become part of people's brains.

2 Robots would become more like humans.

As we try to make robots more human in form, action and thought, could the time come when robots develop feelings that mirror human emotions?

Probability Rating

No one has yet found a way of making a robot that combines machinery with living **tissue**. So while humans may soon become slightly robotic, through the use of computers and artificial body parts, the possibility of machines becoming more like humans is slim.

Freaky future!

Some futurists – called Singularitarians – argue that a peaceful takeover of the world by robots might be a good thing. They believe the robots would be more intelligent and behave more logically than humans, so would probably be better at running things!

You'll eat meat grown in labs

What do you think you'll be eating in 60 years' time? It's possible that burgers and roasts will still be on the menu – but they might come from a very different source. How would you feel about eating meat that's been grown in a laboratory?

▼ Researchers suggest this could be a sustainable way to meet the demand for meat. What else might labs grow in the future?

How would it work?

This really could happen. In fact, lab-grown burgers already have been produced – but it could be a while before your local supermarket is selling them.

But how do you grow a lab-burger? The lab-burger starts with a single meat **cell**. This cell is divided, then the two new cells are fed and grown until they are big enough to divide. This process is repeated over and over again. Soon the collection of cells has grown into a lump of meat. Hey presto – dinner is served!

Would it be a good idea?

People are divided about whether growing food in labs is a good idea. Many animal rights groups feel this is a much more humane way to produce meat, whereas others think it is wrong to modify animal cells in this way as there may be unexpected side effects.

Probability Rating

The land and other resources needed to feed just one person who eats meat can feed at least *six* people who don't. In the future, there will be many more people to feed; farmers may need to use the land to grow crops rather than graze livestock so that we can feed all these people.

In years to come, if you want to eat meat, a laboratory might be the only place you can get it!

▲ Yum, a burger! But what's it doing in a petri dish?

Your food will improve your health

Almost everyone loves ice cream, pizza, fish and chips or sweets. The trouble is they contain lots of fat or sugar – which can lead to health problems if you eat too much. But what if you could pick foods like these for their health *benefits*?

EAT YOUR WAY STRONG WITH

LA SCALA PIZZA!

La Scala pizza looks, smells and tastes like an ordinary pizza, but this pizza actually improves your health. Special ingredients help the body to absorb the nutrients you need most. From extra vitamins in the morning, to extra protein at lunch, La Scala identifies and targets your nutritional needs.

Your toilet and fridge might 'talk'

Wait – there's more. Imagine if your toilet could talk! Doctors have been analysing patients' waste (poo and wee) for centuries to work out what is wrong with them. In the future, toilets might do this job, detecting potential illnesses or analysing deficiencies in your diet. They may even be able to send messages to your fridge, working together to make sure you eat a healthy, balanced diet and get the nutrients you need.

Probability Rating

Scientists now know that the same food can affect different people in different ways. For some people, eating particular foods can increase the likelihood of developing heart disease, diabetes or even cancer.

Experts predict that within a few years, home-testing kits could be available that give you a personal plan of which foods to avoid and which to consume.

The next step may be to target food to help build muscle, lose weight or give you more energy. It could even be possible to give children food that helps them grow taller!

▼ If your toilet detects a lack of calcium in your diet, your fridge may encourage you to eat more yoghurt.

You'll be drinking your own wee

You might be thinking, "I'd rather do anything than drink my own wee!". In the future, though, you might not be able to be so fussy. Many futurists predict that fresh water will one day be so scarce that it will be more precious than oil. We will need to use water from all possible sources – including wee.

NEW

YELLO-WHITE *ON-THE-GO*™!

Never get caught short again!

Are you sick of paying high prices for mineral water? Yello-White's new *On-The-Go*™ **purification** system is the answer!

Simply find a convenient place to wee into the *On-The-Go*™ container. Shake and wait five minutes. Open the spout at the bottom and out pours pure clear water.

How would it work?

You won't have to drink your wee in the state it comes out! We already know how to separate out the water that makes up 95 per cent of urine. All the bad stuff would be **filtered** out.

Would it be a good idea?

There are two big advantages to processing urine as it leaves our bodies:

1. It would make purifying the rest of our waste water simpler and less energy-intensive.
2. If urine was collected, instead of being flushed away, people would flush the toilet less often, saving several litres of water per person, every day.

Probability Rating

Although the amount of fresh water in the world stays the same, the number of people is increasing every year. This means there's less water per person – but instead of using less water, most of us are using more! Water-saving measures will become increasingly important in the future.

It may not be too distant a reality. Astronauts on board the International Space Station already drink their own purified urine.

Other ways wee could save the world

1. Urine contains **phosphate** (used for fertilizers, water softening and as a cleaning agent) which could be extracted and reused.
2. Urine also contains a substance called urea. A scientist has come up with a way of using this to capture carbon dioxide from the atmosphere, reducing greenhouse gases.
3. Some scientists have discovered ways to generate hydrogen fuel from urine, which can be used in specially modified vehicles.

You'll never have to pester your parents for a lift

Isn't it annoying when you want to pop round to see a friend but they live too far away? Everyone's too busy to take you so you end up sitting at home watching rubbish on TV instead. What if you could just jump in a car that would drive you to your friend's house, all by itself?

▲ Why spend time in the car driving? Let the car take care of that, while the driver does something else!

How would it work?

Basically, the car would use sensors to build up a picture of the world around it. The sensors would include cameras, **GPS** and radar, that would relay information to the car's computer about its exact location, nearby objects and what other vehicles and people were doing around it. Based on this, the computer would decide whether or not to turn the wheel, speed up, slow down or stop.

Would it be a good idea?

Driverless cars could give those who cannot drive their own personal and safe form of transport. They would also avoid problems with speeding or dangerous manoeuvres, as restrictions could be programmed into the computer.

But they might not be perfect. If the onboard computer malfunctioned, who would take over? Would there be anyone left in the world with the ability to drive?

▲ This driverless car is being tested in Berlin, Germany. In California, USA, driverless cars are thought to have been involved in just two accidents. One happened when a human was driving, rather than a computer, and the other happened when a human-controlled car drove into the back of the driverless car.

Probability Rating

Driverless cars already exist. In the UK, Heathrow airport has 'personal rapid transport pods' that carry four people and travel at up to 40 kph, though they follow a predetermined route. In the USA, driverless cars have been around since 2012. A fleet of driverless cars have driven themselves safely around the streets of California.

As yet, driverless cars are not available to the general public. Cost is a big factor: the Californian driverless cars cost an additional $150 000, due to the extra equipment they need. However, a large number of companies are working on their own driverless cars, with the hope that we'll all be driving them one day ... or should we say, be driven by them?

You'll blast into space for holidays

Imagine that you've explored the whole world and experienced everything from skiing in the Rockies to scuba-diving off the Australian coast. What you need is a trip to the Moon for a spot of lunar crater racing!

▼ What other activities might a holiday to the Moon promise?

First trips to space

Lots of futurists predict that, based on current trends, people will soon be taking holidays in space. In fact, the world's first-ever space tourist, Dennis Tito, took off in 2001. In May 2012, a spacecraft called *Dragon* made a trip to dock with the International Space Station. Although it was only carrying supplies, it was designed to be able to ferry passengers into space one day. Other companies are developing similar spacecraft, and plan to run space trips very soon.

▼ Is this how we might travel to our holidays in space?

Probability Rating

You may have to wait a while for a trip to the Moon as it is likely most planned passenger flights would only go into sub-orbital space. Although this is technically 'space', the flights may only reach 100 km above the Earth's surface – whereas the Moon is 384 400 km away. More importantly, the cost of flights would be too high for most of us due to the high cost of fuel, expensive technology and repairing damage to the craft. The chances of ordinary people enjoying a space holiday anytime soon are pretty slim!

Freaky future!

Eventually we might all be able to travel further into space, perhaps even to another universe. We might need to travel faster than the speed of light to do so, or perhaps we'd have our bodies frozen, ready to be reawoken when the destination is reached?

You may even be living in space

The world's population is growing rapidly: in 1950 there were 2.5 billion people; in 1999 there were 6 billion; and by 2050 there are forecast to be more than 9 billion. Where will all these people live? Perhaps some of us will have moved to space!

▼ NASA designed colonies for thousands of people within giant spaceships in the 1970s.

How would it work?

In theory a future space **colony** is possible – but there would be some big challenges to overcome:

1. Cost: by 2010, the International Space Station had cost over $100 billion – and it's only about the size of a house. Imagine how much a whole community in space might cost!
2. Food and water: how would we get the water we need to survive in space? How would we grow our food without water and sunlight?
3. Waste disposal: water and waste would need to be recycled or disposed of.
4. Energy: a reliable, safe source of renewable energy, such as solar or nuclear power, would be needed.
5. Air: some way of creating breathable air would have to be found.

▼ What if our space colony is reliant on supplies from Earth, like the space shuttle is now? What happens if supplies can't get through?

Probability Rating

We know it's possible to live in space. People have already spent long periods doing so. The International Space Station has been home to humans since 2000, although it hasn't always been home to the *same* humans – more than 200 people have visited! However, time and money remains an obstacle.

▲ Russian **cosmonaut** Sergei Krikalev has spent a total of more than two years living on the International Space Station!

Thoughts to ponder

Is it possible that we might one day be something other than earthlings? What would we be if we were born far from Earth? How would it change us?

Future bloopers

The predictions in this book are based on what futurists think the world could be like in the next 60 years or more. It might not be a good idea to take them TOO seriously; after all, people have been getting predictions for the future wrong for quite a long time.

THE WORLD WILL BE SHAKEN TO BITS IN … 1982

In the 1970s a book called *The Jupiter Effect*, written by two scientists, predicted that an alignment of the planets on 10th March 1982 would cause a series of terrible earthquakes that would destroy the world.

HALLEY'S COMET WILL KILL US ALL!

This claim in 1910 came after scientists reported that poisonous gas had been detected in the tail of Halley's comet. Worse still, Earth was predicted to pass through the same bit of space as the comet (albeit not at the same time). Sales of gas masks soared, but the danger never materialized.

HUMAN CIVILIZATION WILL DISAPPEAR BY THE YEAR 2000

In 1970, famous US scientist George Wald predicted that, unless immediate action was taken, human civilization would break down in the next 15 to 30 years. Wald was worried that food shortages, conflict over resources, and war would cause the world to descend into chaos.

All computers will crash at 00.00.01 a.m. on 1st January 2000

In 1999, everyone got slightly panicky: would computers be able to cope with the change from dates starting with '19' to dates starting with '20'? What if they all stopped working?

This may not sound like a big problem, but chaos would have ensued if computers had crashed worldwide. Just think of how many crucial services, such as emergency services, air traffic control and banks, depend on computer systems. In the end, though, the 'millennium bug' was fixed in plenty of time.

By 2010, people will live in underwater cities

Visitors to the 1985 FutureWorld exhibition might have come away expecting to be living underwater by 2010. Meanwhile, back up on the surface, everyone would be driving around in solar-powered cars.

Conclusion

It's really difficult to predict how our lives will change in the future. The predictions in this book may turn out to be right or bloopers – only time will tell!

Quiz of your future!

If you could choose how your future would look, what would you choose? Take the quiz and find out which future would be perfect for you.

1. What would you like to do first thing in the morning?

a) Look out at the stars through your space cabin's porthole.

b) Have breakfast in bed (brought to you by your personal robot servant).

c) Blow into a plastic bag to make sure you're still just as healthy as when you went to sleep.

2. Your ideal birthday cake (when you're 60) would be:

a) Made of soybean curd and mushrooms.

b) Something your personal kitchenbot has whisked up.

c) Whatever the computer tells you your body requires, of course. You don't stop being healthy just because it's your birthday!

3. What job do you aim to get?

a) Space farmer.

b) Work? What, the stuff robots do for us?

c) Programmer of health software.

4. Your favourite holiday is:

a) To a space station, or one of the other planets. The only trouble is, they're so far away you have to take two years off …

b) Anywhere, virtually! You just select the destination software, jump into your claytronics suit and put on your 3D goggles.

c) You don't need holidays. You're far too healthy to need a rest, ever.

5. How would you prefer to socialize?

a) You're happy just to meet up with the people who end up on the same space station as you.

b) Hanging out with friends online, maybe pulling on the claytronics suit if there's a virtual party somewhere in the universe to go to.

c) At the gym, when the computer tells you you need to do some exercise.

Turn to page 40 to see what future lies in store …

Glossary

account	a collection of money kept by a bank for a customer
bacteria	a single-celled organism
bamboozle	to confuse
cell	the basic unit of all living things
claytronics	a system which uses computer processes to change the shape of materials
colony	a community of people, often in a previously unsettled area
cosmonaut	a Russian word for an astronaut; someone who travels into space
credit	a system of allowing someone to pay for something later on.
digestion	the process of eating and breaking down food to provide the body with energy and nutrients
filter	to remove impurities
futurist	someone who tries to predict what life will be like in the future
GPS	Global Positioning System, a navigation system using satellites, used in satnav devices
immortal	living forever
implant	an object that is placed inside a person's body, such as a heart pacemaker or a microchip
landfill	a place where rubbish is taken to be covered by soil
malfunction	to go wrong
microprocessor	a single computer chip that does the basic work of a computer
miniaturize	to make tiny
nanobots	tiny, often microscopic, robots
nutrients	foods, or parts of foods, that are good for you
organism	something living, specifically here a single-celled life form
phosphate	a naturally occurring chemical that is vital for plant nutrition. However, too much phosphate can be polluting.
prosthetic	replacing a body part
purification	a system of cleaning so that there is nothing dirty or harmful left
resource	something that people can use. For example, farmland and coal are resources
retina	the membrane at the back of the eye, which collects an image from the lens and sends it to the optic nerve
software	the programs and other operating information used in a computer
spy drone	a pilotless, remote-controlled aircraft with powerful cameras on board
thermal	detecting or retaining heat
tissue	the substance that makes up an organism
trend	a general direction in which something is changing. For example, the current increase in the use of smartphones is a trend.
virtual	1 made by a computer to appear to exist; 2 happening by means of a computer. For example, a virtual classroom is where people in different places share learning via the Internet.

Index

3D goggles 7
3D printing 10–11
BCI (Brain Computer Interface) 19
cars 30–31, 37
claytronics 4–5, 7
clothes 8–9
diseases 14–15, 27
doctors 14–15, 27
drinking water 28–29, 35
food 24–25, 26–27, 35
games 5, 7, 8, 16
greenhouse gases 29
Halley's comet 36
holograms 5
implants 3, 12–13, 18, 19
International Space Station 33, 35
invisibility 9
Jupiter Effect, The 36
meat ("growing") 24–25
memory capacity 18
micro-robots 20–21
microprocessors 12, 13
millennium bug 37
money 12–13

recycling 21, 35
retina scans 13
robots 19, 20–21, 22–23
schools 16–17
smartphones 8, 13
social networks 8, 9
space 32–33, 34–35
spy drones 9
time travel 6–7
virtual learning 16–17
water 25, 28–29, 35

Quiz of your future! – the answers

Mostly a – You'd enjoy a future where humans leave Earth to live in space. Let's just hope you don't get space sick!

Mostly b – Your ideal future is dominated by robots and other technology. Humans spend their time doing as little as possible.

Mostly c – Health concerns are very important in your future. Maybe some disease or catastrophe has caused this change? Or maybe you just want to be the first human to live to be 1000!